# WE LIVE.
# WE LEARN.
# WE SHIFT

## A Journey to Renewed Mind, Heart and Habits

## JUDITH WILSON

**BambuSparks**

First Printing July 2023

Published by:
BambuSparks Publishing
4 Rochester Avenue,
Kingston 8, Jamaica W.I.
www.bambusparks.com

Cover Design: Olivia Designs
Formatting: BambuSparks | www.bambusparks.com

Unless otherwise noted, Scripture quotations are from the Authorized King James
Version of the Bible.

For feedback, bulk orders or speaking engagements, contact the author at
booksbyjudithwilson@gmail.com

*I would like to dedicate this book to all who have experienced some level of mental instability. You are not alone. Be patient with yourself as your mind is being transformed.*

# ACKNOWLEDGEMENTS

I could not conceivably produce this book without acknowledging some key persons who were instrumental in their belief in, and support of, me.

To begin, I want to thank all my friends, who have given me the moral support to write this second book.

Next, I would like to recognize my family who is always telling me how proud they are of me. Much appreciation to them for expressing such confidence in me.

In conclusion, thank you to my publishing team, BambuSparks, located in Kingston, Jamaica, West Indies for their encouragement. Of course, above all, I give thanks to my Creator for this opportunity to share words of encouragement with you.

My heartfelt thanks to all of you.

# ACKNOWLEDGEMENTS

# CONTENTS

# INTRODUCTION

This workbook is designed to empower and inspire you to overcome life's challenges and embrace a future filled with limitless possibilities!

Life can be tough, and we all face our own share of struggles, disappointments, and pain. But let me tell you something: You are not alone on this journey. I have also experienced great sadness, loss, and confusion from being persecuted for who I am. I asked why there is so much evil in the world, looking for an answer that does not seem easy.

I discovered a profound truth in My Problem: There is a higher Power, the Creator, who carefully created us all in his sacred image.
Even if we are sad, he will never forget us. He sends his angels to guide and protect us in times of crisis, even when we are hardly aware of them.

This workbook was born out of my own journey, one that taught me courage, the power of faith, and the incredible power we all have within ourselves. It is a testament to the unwavering support I received from the community and reminds me that we do not have to walk in life alone. Loved ones are happy to hold our hands, hug us with love and walk with us through the stormiest storms.

In these pages you will find the tools, exercises, and guidance you need to change, heal your mind, and develop a positive outlook. It is a method for self-discovery, personal growth, ultimate purpose, and fulfillment in life. We will fight against the lies that hold us back, embrace our unique characters and learn to see ourselves through the eyes of our Creator's love and acceptance.

As you begin this journey of transformation, remember that your Creator has a divine plan for your life. You are wonderful and deserve to overcome any temporary challenge you face.

Embrace your path no matter how hard it is. In times of rest and uncertainty, rely on the Creator's guidance, your inner GPS, to guide you to a victorious future.

I want you to know that you are not alone. Reach out to people who can listen, understand, and support you. Find comfort in prayer, for your Creator is always there, ready to comfort and give you peace. Do not believe the lies that try to deceive or mislead you. You have the ability to overcome your situation: rise above it and create your own destiny.

When using the information in this book, remember that this is just the beginning of your transformation. Every challenge you face is an opportunity to elevate your thinking, and every lesson brings you closer to the person you were created to be. Use the inner strength deposited in you by your Creator to conquer your mind and groom the foundation of your heart for positive change.

Please note that the information shown here is not exhaustive but is important to help you navigate your daily life. It includes practical tools, meditation exercises, and prayers to remind you of your relationship with a loving and caring Heavenly Father.

You are stronger than you think and can change your thoughts, feelings, and behaviors with help from your Creator. Believe in yourself, speak positive words because they have life and be confident about the way forward. I am proud of you and believe in your ability to fight for the good of your heart.

So, my friends, take a deep breath and embark on the incredible adventure of self-discovery and transformation. Use your inner strength, hold on to hope, and let the pages of this book be your guide.

# ABANDONMENT

**Abandonment** – According to the online dictionary, abandonment is "the act of leaving someone or something or of ending or stopping something, usually forever." Abandonment may also be construed to be a state of feeling undesired, discarded, worthless, unprotected, helpless, unsupported, unimportant, unloved, and often comes with a strong sense of betrayal and guilt.

## Thoughts and Feelings of Abandonment

You may feel like no one remembers you or cares about you. You are sad, You may say, "No one cares enough about calling me, considers me to be their friend, or to extend invitations to me for outings. I feel left out, inadequate, and not good enough, or else others would notice me. No one wants to be my friend at school, in my community or at my place of worship. My father, mother, and my siblings have all moved away from me. I have been left to figure life out on my own. I look at my friends, and they have friends and family members who are always inviting them out.

I am not handsome or pretty enough. I do not engage in sports, and do not have the physique like the others. I do not have name-brand.

clothes. I do not use drugs, alcohol, disobey the law, or have illicit sex. These attributes single me out and make me feel like I need to go against my belief system to appease the "status quo."

## Words of Encouragement

You ask yourself the searching question: Is something inherently wrong with me? My answer to you is: No, you are wonderful, just the way you are.

You should also know that your Creator will never forsake or abandon you. You may be feeling forsaken by your friends, but you are not forgotten by your Creator. Adopting habits that are deemed unhealthy is not worth the risk for your health and life.

It is unpleasant to not be acknowledged or celebrated by others. However, in some instances, being excluded from the "in crowd" can be a blessing. It could very well be that you are being protected from harm. If it is that you yearn to have friendships, it would be advantageous for you to seek a well-informed, seasoned person to direct you to people who share your values, or you can take the initiative in discovering them.

I am also recommending that you associate with wholesome community groups, and organizations like a church that teaches character building. You can also be the leader of a group. This way you can then have a more superior sense of the people connecting themselves with you. All in all, endeavor to replace abandonment with perseverance, and pursue renewed friendships.

Look up words of encouragement on your worksheet to replace your thoughts and feelings of abandonment. Feelings transform a cue into an emotion.

## Encouragement from the Bible

Here are some Bible verses to encourage your mind:

**Psalm 27:9-14:** ⁹Hide not thy face far from me, put not thy servant away in anger: thou hast been my help: leave me not, neither forsake me, O God of my salvation. ¹⁰ When my father and my mother forsake me then the Lord will take me up. ¹¹Teach me thy way, O Lord, and lead me in a plain path, because of mine enemies. ¹² Deliver me not over unto the will of mine enemies: for false witnesses are risen up against me, and such as breathe out cruelty. ¹³I had fainted unless I had believed to see the goodness of the Lord in the land of the living. ¹⁴Wait on the Lord: be of good courage and he shall strengthen thine heart: wait I say, on the Lord."

**John 3:16:** "For God so loved the world, that he gave his only begotten Son, that whosoever believeth in him should not perish, but have everlasting life.

**Psalm 23:1-6**: ¹"The LORD is my shepherd; I shall not want. ² He maketh me to lie down in green pastures: he leadeth me beside the still waters.³ He restoreth my soul: he leadeth me in the paths of righteousness for his name's sake. ⁴ Yea, though I walk through the valley of the shadow of death, I will fear no evil: for thou art with me; thy rod and thy staff they comfort me. ⁵ Thou preparest a table before me in the presence of mine enemies: thou anointest my head with oil; my cup runneth over. ⁶ Surely goodness and mercy shall follow me all the days of my life: and I will dwell in the house of the LORD forever. Your Creator will give you everything you need, talk to him. He will never lead you astray!

# Words of Affirmation

God
Is always available to me.

He wonderfully created me.

I will seek positive attention.

I will not always wait for others to reach out to me.

I am not alone.

I have support.

I must change my perspective about myself because I am enough.

I will attempt to create meaningful relationships by extending myself to others.

I will reach out for help to assist me with finding new ways of establishing and maintaining good relationships.

# Prayer for Abandonment

Heavenly Father,
Your Word tells me that you
are always with me. Therefore, I am not alone.

Thank you. I also know that you are mindful of all my needs
today and always. Please help me to continue to trust you no
matter the situation that I face.

# ABUSE

**ABUSE** – is inflicting pain and senseless violence toward another vulnerable person, exerting power and control. The Gale Encyclopedia of Medicine defines abuse as "any action that intentionally harms or injures another person." We are advised, as well, that abuse comes in many forms and is not limited to one gender, culture, or age group. People experience sexual, emotional, psychological, economic, financial, legal, physical, neglect, self-neglect, discrimination, modern slavery, organizational, domestic, abandonment, isolation, and spiritual abuse, to name a few.

## Thoughts and Feelings of Abuse

You have been abused and do not know if you will ever recover from the abuse. Although you did not provoke anyone to inflict pain upon you, you are feeling tremendous guilt, and shame. You are blaming yourself for what was done to you. You may even be afraid of what would happen and how you would be perceived by others if they were to find out about the abuse you are quietly encountering.

Abuse does not define who you are as a person. Do not condemn yourself for what has unfortunately happened to you.

**Words of Encouragement**
Contrary to what some people may say, you do not deserve to be abused by anyone, and you do have the right to live without fear and trepidation. Evil is present around us everywhere, and Satan is always looking to destroy precious souls like yours. Do not give him victory by remaining quiet. I pray that God will give you the courage to share your pain with someone you trust. This trauma can be unbearable at times for you to handle. Cry out to God! He can deliver and restore you.

Do not give your God-given power over to the forces of darkness by allowing your negative experience (s) to dominate your life. In the beginning, you will feel as though you will never rise above this emotional experience: give yourself ample time. Take your time to process the pain, violation, betrayal, anger, distrust, and shock. Do not accuse yourself of the profound trauma someone has intentionally caused you. It will take time to heal and in time, you will heal properly. You will be sufficiently restored, so do not hate yourself. There is support available for you through prayer, counseling, groups, having a trusted person to listen to you share your thoughts and feelings.

If you find yourself stuck and having difficulty moving beyond the abuse, seek professional help. There are many capable, experienced persons available to help you. Also, attempt to make a shift with the words you speak over your life. Speak positively with considerable confidence, genuinely believing and expecting change. Life and death are in the power of your tongue. Be patient with yourself. Over time, healing will take place; however, there must be a willingness on your part, to want to change work through the abuse and not become stuck.

## Encouragement from the Bible

Here are some Bible verses that will encourage your heart.

**Psalm 119:145:** "I cried with my whole heart; hear me, O LORD …"; verse 153, "Consider mine affliction and deliver me …"; verse 161, "Princes have persecuted me without a cause: but my heart standeth in awe of thy word."

**Psalm 143:3:** "For the enemy hath persecuted my soul; he hath smitten my life down to the ground: he hath made me to dwell in darkness, as those that have been long dead."

Your abuse will not go unnoticed by your Creator. You are lovely the way he created you. Rise above your abuse and shine with the proper help to restore things that were stolen from you because of the abuse.

You are precious in God's sight. You are God's jewel because he created you. He made you beautiful and with a purpose. No one has the right to use force toward you that results in bodily, financial, or psychological pain.

# Words of Affirmation

I will not focus on my pain but will rise above it.

I will feed and nourish my mind with positive,

thoughts. I believe I can do all things through,

Christ. I can amid my pain,

therefore, I will be patient,

with myself

I am,

Realizing that

I am stronger than I think,

Because my life is in God's hands

I am not alone or defeated. I am victorious,

and blessed. God will restore me because he

loves me always. He will never leave nor forsake me. No!

As you carefully read these words of affirmation, intentionally allow them to completely penetrate your conscious thoughts. By doing so, your proper perspective about yourself will subtly begin shifting from negative to positive.

# *Prayer for Abuse*

What did I do
to deserve to be enslaved?
I was created in the image and likeness

of my Creator, with purpose. God! Please send me
Destiny Helpers to help me to get out of this pit. I know you can
deliver me, just like you helped the three Hebrew boys to get out of

the fiery furnace. I am in a fiery furnace of abuse; I want to get out.
Please speak to me, God.

# ANGER

**ANGER –** is described as "a strong feeling of displeasure aroused by a wrong."

## Thoughts and Feelings of Anger
I am terribly angry right now at everything, and everyone. I do not know how to adequately control this feeling, or ugly thoughts I invariably have towards myself or others.

## Words of Encouragement
Anger can be turned around by you ruling it and not it, controlling you. If you are finding it difficult to naturally contain your fierce anger, I gently encourage you to constructively engage in a physical activity. For example, go for a walk; jog; locate someone with whom you can openly express your thoughts and feelings; count to ten (10); close your eyes, then take a deep breath in and slowly breathe out; listen to calming music and pray. These are important tools for you to utilize to refocus your thoughts.

Earnest prayer always works. Ask your heavenly Father to help you to control your anger. Also, carefully write your genuine feelings on private paper, then discard it. Naturally, you do not want the written words to get into the wrong hands. A personal journal is useful for this purpose. Occasionally, you can look back at your notes and record your growth.

If you tend to get angry easily, become enraged, and passionate anger typically absorbs your everyday life, I recommend that you quickly ask for professional help. You rightfully deserve to experience peace in your wounded heart, mind, body, and suffering soul. I have generously provided you with a beautiful toolkit with replacement words for pent-up anger. Intentionally incorporate these words into your vocabulary. Intentionally develop and build new habits. Your appropriate response will depend on how motivated you are to make the desired change.

Reach out for needed help if you are unable to carefully control your anger. Critically observe if it is escalating, you are feeling out of control and are becoming abusive to yourself or others.

## Encouragement from the Bible

Here are some Bible verses to help you in stirring your thought process.

**Proverbs 15:1,8:** "A soft answer turneth away wrath but grievous words stir up anger. A wrathful man stirreth up strife but he that is slow to anger appeaseth strife."

Listen attentively before you speak contemptuously.

# Words of Affirmation

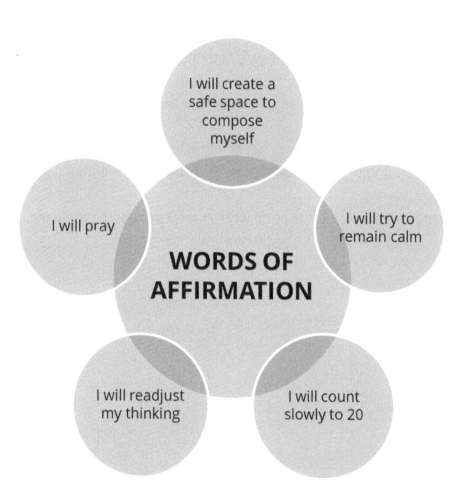

# Prayer for Anger

Heavenly Father,
I confess to you that
sometimes I really feel very angry.

I know that this is not healthy for me and so
I humbly ask you to help me to respond differently.

when I am tempted to respond with anger. I trust you to help me,
and thank you.

# ANXIETY

**ANXIETY –** is defined as a feeling of "distress, or uneasiness of mind, caused by fear or danger, or misfortune." Additionally, anxiety may be described as a feeling of intense uneasiness and overwhelming fear of a threatening situation, place, person, or thing to the point of impairment of your mind, body, and spirit.

## Thoughts and Feelings of Anxiety
My kindred spirit is genuinely troubled, and I am feeling worn down and genuinely distressed. I do not believe I can cope adequately in this stressful situation by carefully adjusting my thinking after experiencing these life-altering events.

## Words of Encouragement
It is natural and normal to feel anxious. You do not need to feel ashamed about your feelings of anxiety. No one knows your life journey and the thing that triggers your anxiety. That said, if you are experiencing frequent and elevated levels of anxiety, it is chronic and immediate help is needed.

You can lead a productive life if given the proper tools, and if you receive the needed help. All humans at some point in their lives feel anxious about issues, whether positive or negative to a lesser or greater degree. Building new habits will be beneficial and should be done intentionally.

The following set of activities will prove to be helpful whenever you experience feelings of anxiety.

1. *Find a quiet spot and sit down*. Close your eyes and breath slowly and deeply. Think about your immediate circumstances and try to identify what is making you feel anxious. Ask yourself what you are going to do about it. Make a list of the course of action that you will commit yourself to take. Close your eyes and breathe slowly and deeply until you feel sufficiently relaxed.

2. **Make yourself a cup of Chamomile Tea**. Create and sit in a quiet, beautiful space with meditative music playing in the background. Visualize a beautiful, peaceful place (i.e., the ocean, rainforest, etc.) while sipping your Tea. You may invite someone to help you process your thoughts if you choose. Tell yourself that you have all the tools that you need to work through this anxiety, and to shift your focus.

Look for an activity that is happening around you in which you can engage. This will shift your thoughts from the anxiety-producing matter(s). Identify and surround yourself with individuals who are understanding and supportive.

If none of these tools are helping you, look at the resource list I have provided at the back of the book and reach out for help. I would also suggest incorporating prayer as part of your daily regimen. Prayer is amazingly effective! It has been documented that prolonged stress is not healthy and could negatively impact your physical, mental, and emotional health. Do not be afraid to reach out for help.

Irrespective of the diverse types of approaches being used to redirect our thinking, it is my firm belief that our Creator knows each one of us and our idiosyncrasies. So, communicating with him will help you through your anxious moments.

## Encouragement from the Bible
**2 Timothy 1:7:** "For God hath not given us the spirit of fear; but of power, and of love, and of a sound mind."

**Isaiah 26:3:** "Thou wilt keep him in perfect peace, whose mind is stayed on thee: because he trusteth in thee."

**Philippians 4:6,7:** [6]"And the peace of God, which passeth all understanding, shall keep your hearts and minds through Christ Jesus. Be careful about nothing; but in everything by prayer and supplication with thanksgiving let your requests be made known unto God."

**Psalm 119:143:** "Trouble and anguish have taken hold on me: yet thy commandments are my delights."

# Words of Affirmation

I am courageous.

I am Smart.

I am an overcomer.

I will not be afraid.

I am strong!

I am an impressive person.

I am different, and this is what makes me special.

I will breathe slowly and think of only good things.

# BULLYING

**BULLYISM** – is said to be the "abuse and mistreatment of someone vulnerable by someone stronger, more powerful..." (Unknown).

Bullying is also an intentional aggressive behavior that causes physical, emotional, and psychological injury to persons a bully perceives to be weaker than them, in all areas of life. The bully additionally employs other methods to negatively impact the life of other persons by coercing them to commit egregious acts against their will. Sequentially, this evokes some sense of superior control in the mind of the bully.

Bullies tend to tease, intimidate, mock, attack, torment, ridicule, trick, oppress, insult, slander, oppress, ridicule, taunt, embarrass, shame, shun, harass, beat up others, and so much more.

## Thoughts and Feelings about Bullying

I have been bullied and am feeling afraid. "I really do not know what to do to prevent others from treating me so unkindly. Maybe I deserve to be bullied.

## Words of Encouragement

I am encouraging you to expose the bully. Do not suffer in silence. Do not allow a bully or anyone to define you. You are not what a bully says that you are. Do not believe the lies.

Keep in mind that a bully is mentally ill. He or she may perceive their targets as threats depending on the level of their mental status. Based on my knowledge of bullies, they perceive themselves to have been wronged. They harbor resentment and hold on to unresolved trauma. Although the purpose of this book is to provide you with useful tools to learn and shift your negative pattern of thinking, it is important to briefly discuss the mindset of a bully in this section since we are highlighting it.

Bullies are hurt people who tend to transfer their hurt to others even more viciously than what they experienced. Your thoughts and feelings about bullying are real and should not be minimized. Tell somebody about what you are experiencing and if necessary, call the authorities.

It is natural to feel the way that you do. However, you should always remind yourself that you are not what anyone claims that you are. Therefore, do not define yourself by the words of a bully. Chances are, he or she wishes to be the person that you are. He or she sees something in you that they do not possess. So, hold your head up high and stand upright. Face your giant because if you do not, it will overpower you. Again, reach out to someone you trust and tell them if you are being bullied. Bullies are cowards!

With God's help, you will overcome and be set free from the shackles of your mind. You are loved with everlasting love by your Creator. Do not be silent!

## Encouragement from the Bible

**Romans 12:19-2** will encourage your heart and mind while you are confronted by this horrible act of bullying.

[19] Dearly beloved, avenge not yourselves, but rather give place unto wrath: for it is written, Vengeance is mine; I will repay, saith the Lord. [20] Therefore if thine enemy hunger, feed him; if he thirsts, give him drink: for in so doing thou shalt heap coals of fire on his head. [21] Be not overcome evil but overcome evil with good.

You will overcome, do not give in, or give up!

# *Prayer for Bullying*

Heavenly Father,
I do feel afraid and lonely
when others bully me; when they
refuse to include me in their activities,

and treat me as though I am a nobody. I confess to you
that I sometimes believe them when they tell me that I am ugly.
I see that your Word says that I was made by you; that you blessed.

me with talents and abilities. Please help me to believe in myself,
and to use the talents and abilities that you have given me.
I thank you for making me, me.

# CHAOS

**CHAOS** - occupying no structure. "A state of utter confusion". Approaching situations and life randomly can trigger a distinct feeling of anxiousness.

## Thoughts and Feelings about Chaos
You are feeling emotional turmoil, out of control, and cannot achieve fundamental tasks, not so much as to thoroughly clean your disordered room. You are feeling deeply overwhelmed and chaotic inside your anxious thoughts.

## Words of Encouragement
Organize your day by getting a calendar, then, create a "To-Do List" that will provide structure and assist you with carefully managing your time. Start by compiling an abbreviated list and ensure that it is used daily. Endeavour to stick to your "To-Do List."

It will also be helpful for you to have a designated place in which to keep things. There is an old adage that says: "There is a place for everything; keep everything in its place" (anonymous).

Another helpful tool is to package and label items that are kept in particular spaces. This will be particularly helpful with respect to your refrigerator. Consider, as well, organizing your closet in terms of items of the respective items of clothing.

## Encouragement from the Bible

Here is a Bible verse to encourage your spirit during this chaotic period of your life.

**Isaiah 26:3:** "Thou wilt keep him in perfect peace, whose mind is stayed on thee: because he trusteth in thee." Preoccupy your mind with things that are lovely and calming.

Our lives can feel like this toolbox at times, confusing, chaotic with many tools that are good to use but difficult to find the right one because of the disorganization of our mind. We must be patient and diligent in our pursuit to find the right tool we need in the moment. While you are doing so, pray.

# Prayer for Chaos

My Creator
and ruler of everything,
I come before you now asking

for help. Everything feels like they are
spinning out of control, total chaos. I need you
to help because I cannot function without you. Grant me

the mental strength to my thoughts and environment.

# DESPAIR

**DESPAIR** – According to the Merriam-Webster Dictionary, despair is "Utter loss of hope." Despair can also be described as a feeling of hopelessness and defeat.

## Thoughts and Feelings about Despair

If you are in despair, all is not lost. You may not know what to do or where to go. Life perhaps does not make any sense. I can relate. Since the loss of my mother, life has not been the same. She was the only one that I had. She was my go-to person; my rock; my support.

When you are in despair, your spirit is deeply sad, which in turn affects your thought process and your mood, which lowers your self-esteem. You experience feelings of hopelessness and loss of interest in activities or things you once enjoyed. You feel like no one remembers you, or cares about you. No one seems to consider you to be their friend, or to extend invitations to you for outings. You feel left out, inadequate, and not good enough to be noticed by others.

You perceive that no one wants to be your friend at school, in your community, or at your place of worship. The members of your family have all moved away from you. You have been left to figure life out on your own and this makes you feel angry, anxious, and sad. You look at your friends, and they have friends all around them, parents loving them, and people are always inviting them out. Yet, no one calls you. Not only that, but you also believe you are not handsome or pretty, or cool enough. You do not use drugs, alcohol, disobey the law, have illicit sex, and you do not have the physique like the others. You often ask yourself this question, "What is wrong with me?"

## Words of Encouragement

Those of you who might be using drugs, seek help. This is dangerous to your entire body, mind, and spirit. You are no longer operating on a conscious level and you are unable to function as the person you were created to be. Pray and ask your Creator to help you and seek professional help immediately.

Positive reinforcements are good to complete the new habit cycle, therefore, a shift in unfavorable thinking to positive thoughts will result in positive outcomes. As you consistently replace negative thoughts with positive ones, your new pattern of thinking will likely be strengthened.

## Encouragement from the Bible

Here is a Bible verse to encourage you on your journey.

**Psalm 30:5:** "For His anger endureth but a moment, and in His favor is life; weeping may endure for a night, but joy cometh in the morning.

**2 Corinthians 4:8,16,17,18:** [8] We are troubled on every side, yet not distressed; we are perplexed, but not in despair; ... [16] For which cause we faint not; but though our outward man perish, yet the inward man is renewed day by day. [17] For our light affliction, which is but for a moment, worketh for us a far more exceeding and eternal weight of glory; [18] While we look not at the things which are seen, but at the things which are not seen: for the things which are seen are temporal; but the things which are not seen are eternal.

The one who created you is bigger than your problems and he truly cares about your concerns. Talk to him about matters that trouble your heart and mind.

**Deuteronomy 31:8:** "And the Lord, he it is that doth go before thee; he will be with thee, he will not fail thee, neither forsake thee: fear not, neither be dismayed."

# Words of Affirmation

Read, believe, and act on these words:

I will stop to smell the roses/flowers today. I am brave; I am accomplished. I am smart. I am successful.

I will show gratitude for persons, places, and things that I have been blessed with by my Creator.

Today, I will not focus on my feelings and thoughts. Instead, I will give thanks for the things that are going well in my life.

Give thanks to your Creator, no matter how hard you may think it is. Our Creator promised that he will NEVER leave nor forsake us.

Wow! This is good news, so you can run to him for everything you need. When you are sad, he will make you glad.

He will be my friend when everyone is gone around me. He is like no other. This is the reason I love and adore him.

When everyone is busy with their own challenges, I can run to my God, Creator, Friend, Confidante, and Counselor.

I gain wisdom, knowledge, clarity, and truth from reading his WORD and talking to him. I encourage you to do the same; you will not be disappointed.

I also encourage you to include laughter in your daily life. Infect others with laughter. It is free, natural, and contagious.

# SHAME

**SHAME** – can be defined as a feeling of inferiority or unworthiness (Merriam-Webster Dictionary).

## Thoughts and Feelings of Shame

After all of what happened, I really don't know how I am going to get out of the house and face anyone. I will not be able to manage the stares and the whispers from those around me. Before all this, everyone looked up to me; I was respected in the community. Now, I don't think that I can live this one down. If only it had never happened.

## Words of Encouragement

You are not defined by the defamatory words that are spoken against you. You are vicariously experiencing these negative feelings because another human being has willfully violated you. You may have also made poor choices that have inadvertently brought you emotional pain and shame. You are feeling downcast and thinking you cannot be generously forgiven for the activities you have been engaged in to deflate your once powerful sense of self. There is no circumstance under the brilliant sun and nothing you have done that cannot be forgiven if you want to change course.

With God's help, you will overcome and be set free from the shackles of your mind. You are loved unconditionally with an everlasting love by your Creator. You are courageous, stronger than you think, smart, fun, confident, prayerful, and unselfish. Get up! Move your body, do something, Jumping Jax, dance, step exercise, jump rope, run up and down the stairs. jump in place, stretch your limbs.

## Encouragement from the Bible
This Bible passage will undoubtedly encourage your anxious heart.

**Psalm 25:1-3:** "Unto thee, O LORD, do I lift up my soul. ²O my God, I trust in thee: let me not be ashamed, let not mine enemies triumph over me. ³ Yea, let none that wait on thee be ashamed: let them be ashamed which transgress without cause." Jesus bore your shame so that you do not have to carry it around.

# Words of Affirmation

I am doing great!

I am worthy of God's grace and love.

I am on the right track.

I will have a conversation with my Creator today, he is waiting to hear my voice.

I am not alone.

I will pray daily.

I am a beautiful soul.

I will rise above my pain.

I am better than my hurt.

I am not crazy.

I am victorious.

I am triumphant.

I am an overcomer. I am not a victim.

I am perfect just the way I was created.

I will be intentional about using positive words to retrain my brain.

# Prayer for Shame

Heavenly Father,
I am so very glad that I belong to you.
I am yours.
You are not ashamed to call me your child.

I am also very glad that
I can talk to you about this shameful thing that happened to me.

Please help me to get over it and give me the courage to go on.
Thank you.

# WORKSHEETS

In this section, there are worksheets on each topic you have read about. On each worksheet, write your thoughts down and use them as a tool to shift your thinking.

# ABUSE WORKSHEET #1

Date: _____

My Initial Thoughts About Abuse:

_____

_____

_____

_____

_____

_____

_____

_____

_____

_____

_____

_____

_____

_____

Date: _____

My Thoughts After Using the Toolkit:

_____

_____

_____

_____

_____

_____

_____

_____

_____

_____

_____

_____

_____

_____

_____

_____

_____

_____

# ABUSE WORKSHEET #2

WRITE YOUR SUCCESS
Which tool did you take from the toolkit?

_____

_____

_____

_____

_____

_____

_____

_____

How did I use this tool to overcome your negative feelings and thoughts?

_____

_____

_____

_____

_____

I am proud of myself for successfully using the tools in my thoughts and feelings toolkit. I will treat myself to something healthy, share the good news with someone who has my best interest at heart.

Write down how or what you will do to celebrate this milestone.

_____

_____

_____

_____

_____

_____

_____

_____

_____

_____

_____

_____

_____

_____

We are all connected, and the lessons we learn in life should not be kept to ourselves. It is imperative that we help each other by imparting what we have learned in our life's journey to those we may encounter who are experiencing the same challenges. I am sharing with you with the expectation that you will also share.

# ANGER WORKSHEET 1

Date: _____

My Initial Thoughts About Anger:

_____

_____

_____

_____

_____

_____

_____

_____

_____

_____

_____

_____

_____

_____

_____

_____

_____

_____

My tongue has life, and I will speak about the things I want to see happening, the change in my life, and believe it. Pray!

I used the tools in the toolkit to overcome negative thoughts today. This is cause for celebration. I am resilient and acknowledge I do not give myself enough credit in managing my feelings and thoughts. I am immensely proud of myself today.

Date: _____

## My Thoughts After Using the Toolkit:

_____

_____

_____

_____

_____

_____

_____

_____

_____

_____

_____

_____

_____

_____

_____

_____

_____

_____

_____

_____

# ANGER WORKSHEET #2

WRITE YOUR SUCCESS
Which tool did you take from the toolkit?

_____

_____

_____

_____

_____

_____

_____

_____

_____

_____

_____

_____

_____

_____

_____

How did I use this tool to overcome your negative feelings and thoughts?

_____

_____

_____

_____

_____

_____

_____

_____

_____

_____

_____

_____

_____

_____

_____

_____

_____

I am proud of myself for successfully using the tools in my thoughts and feelings toolkit. I will treat myself to something healthy, share the good news with someone who has my best interest at heart. Write down how or what you will do to celebrate this milestone.

_____

_____

_____

_____

_____

_____

_____

_____

_____

_____

We are all connected, and the lessons we learn in life should not be kept to ourselves. It is imperative that we help each other by imparting what we have learned in our life's journey with those we may encounter that are experiencing the same challenges. I am sharing with you the expectation that you will also share with others.

Talk to God today, right now!

Tell him how you are feeling – he is a great listener.

# ANXIETY WORKSHEET #1

Check inside the boxes to see what you can throw out to free yourself from anxiety.

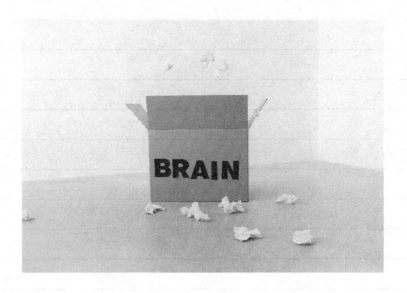

Date: _____

My Initial Thoughts About Anxiety:

_____

_____

_____

_____

_____

_____

_____

_____

_____

_____

_____

_____

_____

_____

_____

_____

_____

_____

Date: _____

My Thoughts After Using the Toolkit:

_____

_____

_____

_____

_____

_____

_____

_____

_____

_____

_____

_____

_____

_____

_____

_____

_____

_____

My Creator has carved and designed me just the way he intended, and I am perfect in every way. I will have a conversation with my Creator today; he is waiting to hear my voice. To hear his voice, find a quiet place that is free of distraction. Close your eyes, clear your mind of everything and everyone around you. To begin your journey, get headphones to block out the noise.

You are in the presence of your Creator and must show reverence to him. Tell him what is going on with you and that you want the situation to turn around for the better. While you are communicating with your Creator, visualize the change you want in your life. This is called Faith in Action. You are calling forth the things that are not now, as though they are.

This should be a daily occurrence. After making your request known to your Creator, start thanking him for meeting your need. Your mind, feelings, and thoughts do not control you; you control them with the guidance, wisdom and help of your Creator. We lack many things because we do not activate our faith, believing that all things are possible.

We shall receive by believing all things are possible when we pray. Pray with expectation and live humbly before your Creator. Work toward letting go of your defeating thoughts; they will cause you to lose all your blessings. When you get blessed, share the blessings in turn with others. Remember, we are all interconnected, and we need each other.

# ANXIETY WORKSHEET #2

Date: _____

My Initial Thoughts About Anxiety:

_____

_____

_____

_____

_____

_____

_____

_____

_____

_____

_____

_____

_____

_____

Date: _____

My Thoughts After Using the Toolkit:

_____

_____

_____

_____

_____

_____

_____

_____

_____

_____

_____

_____

*I am courageous. I am resilient and acknowledge that I do not give myself enough credit in managing my feelings and thoughts.*

A joyful heart is good medicine for my body, mind, and soul. I will show gratitude by giving thanks for being present today. I will have a conversation with my Creator today, he is waiting to hear my voice.

# TOOLS TO MANAGE AND TRANSFORM YOUR THINKING

# TOOLBOX INSPIRATIONAL THOUGHTS

1. From **Abandoned** to - I will remind myself that I am never alone

2. From **Abused** to - I am feeling confident to advocate for myself

3. From **Anger** to - I have a sense of calmness and peace

4. From **Anxiety** to - easiness in my approach to people and situations I perceive to be challenging

5. From **Bullying** to - I will speak up now because I feel empowered

6. From **Chaos** to - I have clarity now about this situation

7. From **Despair** to - I will trust the process, by being hopeful and believing my situation will get better

8. **From Shame** to - I will shift my thinking and develop a new and healthy perspective of myself

9. I will approach challenges with confidence

10. I will rise above the limitations of my mind

11. I will rise above my challenges and naysayers

**REPLACEMENT WORDS**

recognized, supported, empowered, validated, encouraged, affirmed, confident, fearless, hopeful, calm, settled, approved, strong, secure, relieved, escaped, forbearance, pleasure, calmness, patience, relief, tranquility, peace, comfort, sereneness, consolation, contentment, resolved, steadfast, determined, flexible, kind, accepting, tolerant, gentle, merciful, orderliness, order, plan, method, pattern, consistency, resolved, optimistic, lighthearted, joyful, exhilarated, jovial, elated, respected, appreciated, esteemed, honorable.

# Laughter Toolkit

Here a few jokes to make you laugh:

**JOKE 1** - Where did the night go?
**Answer**: To another country

**JOKE 2** - Are you hungry?
**Answer:** I can tell because you are eating your words

Okay, did you laugh?
If you did not, why not? Did you say my jokes were lame, or corny? Well, that in and of itself is funny. I am glad you are rolling your eyes and think that the jokes are dry. That is the joke; the dryness.

## Encouragement from the Bible
**Proverbs 17:22:** "A merry heart doeth good like a medicine: but a broken spirit drieth the bones." It is good to laugh to take your mind off negative thoughts and feelings.

## Words of Encouragement
Having a joyful heart lifts the spirit and is good medicine for the soul. A sorrowful heart infects your spirit, dries up your bones, and leaves you feeling disheartened and dry to your core. Open yourself to laughter.

# ANXIETY WORKSHEET #3

WRITE YOUR SUCCESS

Which tool did you take from the toolkit?

_____

_____

_____

_____

_____

_____

_____

_____

_____

_____

_____

_____

_____

_____

_____

_____

_____

How did I use this tool to overcome your negative feelings and thoughts?

_____

_____

_____

_____

_____

_____

_____

_____

_____

_____

_____

_____

_____

_____

_____

_____

_____

_____

_____

I am proud of myself for successfully using the tools in my thoughts and feelings toolkit to shift my thought process to achieve a positive outcome. I will treat myself to something healthy and share the good news with someone who has my best interest at heart. Write down what you did, the tool you used in your toolkit and how you will celebrate this milestone.

---

---

---

---

---

---

---

---

---

---

---

---

---

---

---

---

---

# BULLYING WORKSHEET 1

Date: _____

My Initial Thoughts About Despair:

_____

_____

_____

_____

_____

_____

_____

_____

_____

_____

_____

_____

_____

_____

_____

_____

_____

_____

Date: _____

My Thoughts After Using the Toolkit:

_____

_____

_____

_____

_____

_____

_____

_____

_____

_____

_____

_____

_____

_____

_____

_____

_____

_____

_____

_____

# BULLYING WORKSHEET #2

WRITE YOUR SUCCESS
Which tool did you take from the toolkit?

_____

_____

_____

_____

_____

_____

_____

_____

_____

_____

_____

_____

_____

How did I use this tool to overcome your negative feelings and thoughts?

_____

_____

_____

_____

_____

_____

_____

_____

_____

_____

_____

_____

_____

_____

_____

_____

_____

_____

_____

_____

I am proud of myself for successfully using the tools in my thoughts and feelings toolkit to shift my thought process to achieve a positive outcome. I will treat myself to something healthy and share the good news with someone who has my best interest at heart. Write down what you did, the tool you used in your toolkit and how you will celebrate this milestone.

_____

_____

_____

_____

_____

_____

_____

_____

_____

_____

_____

_____

We are all connected, and the lessons we learn in life should not be kept to ourselves. It is imperative that we help each other by imparting what we have learned in our life's journey to those encountering the same challenge. I implore you to share how you have overcome this challenge with others.

# CHAOS WORKSHEET #1

Date: _____

My Initial Thoughts About Chaos:

_____

_____

_____

_____

_____

_____

_____

_____

_____

_____

_____

_____

_____

_____

_____

_____

Date: _____

My Thoughts After Using the Toolkit:

_____

_____

_____

_____

_____

_____

_____

_____

_____

_____

_____

_____

_____

_____

I do not give myself enough credit for managing my thoughts and affairs.

# CHAOS WORKSHEET #2

WRITE YOUR SUCCESS
Which tool did you take from the toolkit?

_____

_____

_____

_____

_____

_____

_____

_____

_____

_____

_____

_____

_____

Work at your pace by taking one step at a time. Know your limits and not what others think your limits are or should be. Living up to others' expectations can bring chaos to your mind, especially if you are not strong mentally and grounded.

How did I use this tool to overcome your negative feelings and thoughts?

_____

_____

_____

_____

_____

_____

_____

_____

_____

_____

_____

_____

_____

_____

_____

_____

_____

_____

I am proud of myself for successfully using the tools in my thoughts and feelings toolkit to shift my thought process to achieve a positive outcome. I will treat myself to something healthy and share the good news with someone who has my best interest at heart.

Write down what you did, the tool you used in your toolkit and how you will celebrate this milestone.

_____

_____

_____

_____

_____

_____

_____

_____

_____

_____

_____

_____

_____

_____

_____

I implore you to share how you have overcome this challenge with others. Have a conversation with your Creator today, he is waiting to hear your voice. To hear his voice, it is important to find a place that is quiet and free of distraction. Close your eyes, clear your mind of everything and everyone around you. To begin your journey, get headphones to block out the noise. You are in the presence of your Creator and must show reverence to him. Tell him what is going on with you and that you want the situation to turn around for the better. While you are communicating with your Creator, visualize the change you want in your life. This is called Faith in Action. You are calling forth the things that are not now, as though they are.

This should be a daily occurrence. After making your request known to your Creator, start thanking him for granting this need. Your mind, feelings and thoughts do not control you; you control them with the guidance, wisdom and help of your Creator. We lack many things because we do not activate our Faith, believing that all things are possible. We shall receive by believing all things are possible when we pray. Pray with expectation and live humbly before your Creator.

Work towards letting go of your defeating thoughts; they will cause you to lose all your blessings. Also, when you are blessed, share your blessings in whatever form it comes. Remember, we are all interconnected, and we need each other.

# DESPAIR WORKSHEET #1

"Casting down imaginations, and every high thing that exalteth itself against the knowledge of God and bringing into captivity every thought to the obedience of Christ" (2 Corinthians 10:5).

Date: _____

My Initial Thoughts About Feelings of Despair:

_____

_____

_____

_____

_____

_____

_____

_____

_____

_____

_____

_____

_____

_____

_____

_____

# DESPAIR WORKSHEET #2

Write Your Success

Which tool did you take from the Worksheet?

_____

_____

_____

_____

_____

_____

_____

_____

_____

_____

_____

_____

_____

_____

_____

How did I use this tool to overcome your negative feelings and thoughts?

_____

_____

_____

_____

_____

_____

_____

_____

I am proud of myself for successfully using the tools in my thoughts and feelings toolkit to shift my thought process to achieve a positive outcome. I will treat myself to something healthy and share the good news with someone who has my best interest at heart. Write down what you did, the tool you used in your toolkit and how you will celebrate this milestone. I am a winner!

_____

_____

_____

_____

_____

_____

_____

_____

# SHAME WORKSHEET #1

"Casting down imaginations, and every high thing that exalteth itself against the knowledge of God and bringing into captivity every thought to the obedience of Christ" (2 Corinthians 10:5).

Date: _____

My Initial Thoughts About Shame:

_____

_____

_____

_____

_____

_____

_____

_____

_____

_____

_____

Date: _____

My Thoughts After Using the Worksheet:

_____

_____

_____

_____

_____

_____

_____

_____

_____

_____

_____

_____

I do not give myself enough credit in managing my thoughts and affairs.

A joyful heart is good medicine for my body, mind, and soul. I will show gratitude by giving thanks for being present today. I will have a conversation with my Creator today, he is waiting to hear my voice.

# SHAME WORKSHEET #2

I used the tools in the toolkit to overcome negative thoughts today. This is cause for celebration. I am resilient and acknowledge that I do not give myself enough credit in managing my feelings and thoughts. I am immensely proud of myself today.

WRITE YOUR SUCCESS
*Which tool did you take from the worksheet?*

_____

_____

_____

_____

_____

_____

_____

_____

_____

_____

_____

_____

_____

_____

How did I use this tool to overcome your negative feelings and thoughts?

_____

_____

_____

_____

_____

_____

_____

_____

_____

_____

_____

_____

_____

_____

_____

_____

_____

_____

_____

_____

_____

_____

# AFFIRMATION WORKSHEET

Add your own words of affirmation on this page. This is your space.

_____

_____

_____

_____

_____

_____

_____

Date: _____

My Initial Thoughts Before Using My Own Toolkit:

_____

_____

_____

_____

_____

_____

Date: _____

Thoughts After Using the Worksheet:

_____

_____

_____

_____

_____

_____

_____

_____

_____

_____

_____

_____

_____

Your Creator gave you a voice, use it! Do not allow your adversary to intimidate you. Do not fall into your enemy's trap or for his tricks; he is fighting to snuff your life out. This is his job, to tell you lies about your present and past struggles. He crowds your mind with garbage, rotten thoughts, stinking thinking about who you are.

Replace negative words with positive thoughts about your life. Staying bound will give victory to the one(s) who has harmed you, so get up. Do not give them the pleasure of seeing you down, stuck, unproductive, or giving up on your life. There is hope because you are breathing. You were created beautiful inside and out.

This has not changed; some individuals have created a detour in your path. You will rise and start living again.

# CELEBRATION NOTES #1

I am proud of myself for successfully using the tools in my thoughts and feelings toolkit. I will treat myself to something healthy, share the good news with someone who has my best interest at heart.

Write down how or what you will do to celebrate this milestone.

_____

_____

_____

_____

_____

_____

_____

_____

_____

_____

_____

_____

_____

_____

# CELEBRATION NOTES #2

I used the tools in the toolkit to overcome negative thoughts today. This is cause for celebration. I am resilient and acknowledge that I do not give myself enough credit in managing my feelings and thoughts. I am immensely proud of myself today.

WRITE YOUR SUCCESS
Which tool did you take from the Worksheet?

_____

_____

_____

_____

_____

_____

_____

_____

_____

_____

_____

_____

How did I use this tool to overcome your negative feelings and thoughts?

_____

_____

_____

_____

_____

_____

_____

_____

_____

_____

_____

_____

_____

_____

_____

_____

_____

_____

_____

_____

_____

_____

I am proud of myself for successfully using the tools in my thoughts and feelings toolkit. I will treat myself to something healthy, share the good news with someone who has my best interest at heart.

Write down how or what you will do to celebrate this milestone.

_____

_____

_____

_____

_____

_____

_____

_____

_____

_____

_____

_____

We are all connected, and the lessons we learn in life should not be kept to ourselves. It is imperative that we help each other by imparting what we have learned in our life journey with those we may encounter that are experiencing the same challenges. I am sharing with you, with the expectation that you will also share with others.

# CELEBRATION NOTES #3

I used the tools in the toolkit to overcome negative thoughts today. This is cause for celebration. I am resilient and acknowledge that I do not give myself enough credit in managing my feelings and thoughts. I am immensely proud of myself today.

WRITE YOUR SUCCESS
Which tool did you take from the Worksheet?

_____

_____

_____

_____

_____

_____

How did I use this tool to overcome your negative feelings and thoughts?

_____

_____

_____

_____

_____

_____

I am proud of myself for successfully using the tools in my thoughts and feelings toolkit. I will treat myself to something healthy, share the good news with someone who has my best interest at heart.

Write down how or what you will do to celebrate this milestone.

_____

_____

_____

_____

_____

_____

_____

_____

_____

_____

We are all connected and the lessons we learn in life should not be kept to ourselves. It is imperative that we help each other by imparting what we have learned in our life journey with those we may encounter that are experiencing the same challenges. I am sharing with you the expectation that you will also share with others.

# PRAISE WORKSHEET

Today is a day of praise. Think of a happy moment, space or place in your life, no matter how brief. It could be a smile from someone, someone's laughter, or your own time of joyfulness. Sing seven songs of connectedness to your Creator: songs that will positively uplift your spirit. Songs that will draw from a deep place with your Creator.

**Tell yourself:** I am going to sing seven songs daily starting right now. Sing until you can feel a positive shift in your mind (emotion). Talk to your Creator after you sing your songs of praise. In fact, you can do it simultaneously.

Date: _____

My Initial Thoughts About Praise:

_____

_____

_____

_____

_____

_____

Date: _____

Thoughts After Using the Worksheet

_____

_____

_____

_____

_____

_____

_____

._____

_____

_____

_____

_____

I am doing great! I will have a conversation with my Creator today, he is waiting to hear my voice.

# CELEBRATION NOTES

I used the tools in the toolkit to overcome negative thoughts today. This is cause for celebration. I am resilient and acknowledge I do not give myself enough credit in managing my feelings and thoughts.

I am immensely proud of myself today.

WRITE YOUR SUCCESS
Which tool did you take from the toolkit?

_____

_____

_____

_____

_____

_____

_____

_____

_____

_____

_____

How did I use this tool to overcome your negative feelings and thoughts?

_____

_____

_____

_____

_____

_____

_____

_____

_____

_____

_____

_____

_____

_____

_____

I am proud of myself for successfully using the tools in my thoughts and feelings toolkit. I will treat myself to something healthy, share the good news with someone who has my best interest at heart.

Write down how or what you will do to celebrate this milestone.

_____

_____

_____

_____

_____

_____

_____

_____

_____

_____

_____

_____

We are all connected and the lessons we learn in life should not be kept to ourselves. It is imperative that we help each other by imparting what we have learned in our life journey with those we may encounter that are experiencing the same challenges. I am sharing with you the expectation that you will also share with others.

# CELEBRATION NOTES

I used the tools in the toolkit to overcome negative thoughts today. This is cause for celebration. I am resilient and acknowledge I do not give myself enough credit in managing my feelings and thoughts.
I am immensely proud of myself today.

WRITE YOUR SUCCESS
Which tool did you take from the toolkit?

_____

_____

_____

_____

_____

_____

_____

_____

_____

How did I use this tool to overcome your negative feelings and thoughts?

_____

_____

_____

_____

_____

_____

_____

_____

_____

_____

_____

_____

_____

_____

_____

_____

I am proud of myself for successfully using the tools in my thoughts and feelings toolkit. I will treat myself to something healthy, share the good news with someone who has my best interest at heart.

Write down how or what you will do to celebrate this milestone.

_____

_____

_____

_____

_____

_____

_____

_____

_____

_____

_____

_____

_____

_____

_____

We are all connected and the lessons we learn in life should not be kept to ourselves. It is imperative that we help each other by imparting what we have learned in our life journey with those we may encounter that are experiencing the same challenges. I am sharing with you the expectation that you will also share with others.

# CELEBRATION NOTES

I used the tools in the toolkit to overcome negative thoughts today. This is cause for celebration. I am resilient and acknowledge I do not give myself enough credit in managing my feelings and thoughts.
I am immensely proud of myself today.

WRITE YOUR SUCCESS
Which tool did you take from the toolkit?

_____

_____

_____

_____

_____

_____

_____

_____

_____

_____

How did I use this tool to overcome your negative feelings and thoughts?

_____

_____

_____

_____

_____

_____

_____

_____

_____

_____

_____

_____

_____

_____

_____

I am proud of myself for successfully using the tools in my thoughts and feelings toolkit. I will treat myself to something healthy (.......), share the good news with someone who has my best interest at heart.

Write down how or what you will do to celebrate this milestone.

_____

_____

_____

_____

_____

_____

_____

_____

_____

_____

_____

We are all connected and the lessons we learn in life should not be kept to ourselves. It is imperative that we help each other by imparting what we have learned in our life journey with those we may encounter that are experiencing the same challenges. I am sharing with you the expectation that you will also share with others.

# CELEBRATION NOTES

I used the tools in the toolkit to overcome negative thoughts today. This is cause for celebration. I am resilient and acknowledge I do not give myself enough credit in managing my feelings and thoughts.
I am immensely proud of myself today.

WRITE YOUR SUCCESS
Which tool did you take from the toolkit?

_____

_____

_____

_____

_____

_____

How did I use this tool to overcome your negative feelings and thoughts?

_____

_____

_____

_____

_____

_____

_____

_____

_____

_____

_____

_____

_____

_____

_____

_____

_____

_____

_____

_____

_____

_____

_____

I am proud of myself for successfully using the tools in my thoughts and feelings toolkit. I will treat myself to something healthy, share the good news with someone who has my best interest at heart.

Write down how or what you will do to celebrate this milestone.

_____

_____

_____

_____

_____

_____

_____

_____

_____

_____

_____

_____

_____

We are all connected and the lessons we learn in life should not be kept to ourselves. It is imperative that we help each other by imparting what we have learned in our life journey with those we may encounter that are experiencing the same challenges. I am sharing with you the expectation that you will also share with others.

# CELEBRATION NOTES

I used the tools in the toolkit to overcome negative thoughts today. This is cause for celebration. I am resilient and acknowledge I do not give myself enough credit in managing my feelings and thoughts.
I am immensely proud of myself today.

WRITE YOUR SUCCESS
Which tool did you take from the toolkit?

_____

_____

_____

_____

_____

_____

How did I use this tool to overcome your negative feelings and thoughts?

_____

_____

_____

_____

_____

I am proud of myself for successfully using the tools in my thoughts and feelings toolkit. I will treat myself to something healthy, share the good news with someone who has my best interest at heart.

Write down how or what you will do to celebrate this milestone.

_____

_____

_____

_____

_____

_____

_____

_____

We are all connected and the lessons we learn in life should not be kept to ourselves. It is imperative that we help each other by imparting what we have learned in our life journey with those we may encounter that are experiencing the same challenges. I am sharing with you the expectation that you will also share with others.

# CELEBRATION NOTES

I used the tools in the toolkit to overcome negative thoughts today. This is cause for celebration. I am resilient and acknowledge that I do not give myself enough credit for managing my feelings and thoughts.

I am immensely proud of myself today.

WRITE YOUR SUCCESS
Which tool did you take from the toolkit?

_____

_____

_____

_____

_____

How did I use this tool to overcome your negative feelings and thoughts?

_____

_____

_____

_____

_____

I am proud of myself for successfully using the tools in my thoughts and feelings toolkit. I will treat myself to something healthy, share the good news with someone who has my best interest at heart.

Write down how or what you will do to celebrate this milestone.

_____

_____

_____

_____

_____

_____

_____

_____

We are all connected and the lessons we learn in life should not be kept to ourselves. It is imperative that we help each other by imparting what we have learned in our life journey with those we may encounter that are experiencing the same challenges. I am sharing with you the expectation that you will also share with others.

# CONGRATULATIONS

You have done yourself much good for having applied the tools that are recommended in this book to help you shift your thoughts from the negative to the positive. Well done!

In this section, I encourage you to look within yourself and find your own tools that you can use to help you remain on a positive path. Document your thoughts on the worksheets over the next seven days.

# SIMPLE PRAYERS
# FOR THOSE WHO HAVE NEVER PRAYED

You might be quietly telling yourself that you have never prayed and do not know how to pray. First, let me begin by giving you a brief overview of prayer.

## What is prayer?

It is a conversation between you and the Supreme Being, God, Yahweh your Creator.

Prayer is simply talking to God. You approach him just the way you are because he knows you. Talk to him, then wait and listen to hear what he has to say to you. You are activating a rapport with God, and having a conversation with Him is an act of reverence (respect). Use words that are direct and intentional when you pray. You pray to ask for forgiveness, restoration, direction, wisdom, inspiration, clarity, protection, peace, covering, and things that you need.

You also pray to worship God for who He is, and to praise Him for what He does. Give thanks to him for what He provides.

## Why is it important to pray?

It keeps you focused and centered on the characteristics of your Creator. It also allows you to be still, to hear from the only one who loves you unconditionally. If you have never prayed before, here are a few simple and straightforward ways of talking to your Creator.

114

# Prayer #1:

## *Uncertain of What to Say*

Dear God/Yahweh/My Creator,

I am coming to you today; this is my first time talking to you, one to one. I really do not know what to say to you. I guess I will start by saying thank you for who you are. Thank you for sparing my life from abuse, trauma, cruelty, death, sickness (**fill in the blank**). Thank you also for keeping my mind intact, although sometimes I wonder if it is still with me. I hear that you have a sense of humor, so that was a moment of laughter. I am asking you to watch over me as I go through this day. God, I need you right now, please help me! I am feeling (insert **your emotions here**). So let it be.

# *Prayer #2*
## *For Those Who Are Hurting*

Dear God/Yahweh/My Creator,

I need you right now!
My heart is sad and lonely, my mind is confused, and there is so much chaos and turmoil around me. Are you there? I need you because I do not have the strength to go the distance. Please, God! Guide me, talk to me because I have nothing to look forward to in my life. I have heard that you came through for other people. I need you to come through for me because I am so confused; I don't really know what I want. Please help me, guide me, and give me peace of mind. I really need you to work on my behalf. I have only you to depend on totally. Raise up wholesome, genuine, God-loving people around me. Keep the wolves in sheep's clothing away from me. You just heard my prayer, so I am going to act on what I ask you to do. I am activating my faith. I cannot see or know how you are going to turn my situation around, but I trust you. Thank you for hearing from me. So let it be.

## *Prayer #3:*
# Feeling Overwhelmed

Dear God/Yahweh/My Creator,

I am often overcome by feelings or thoughts of (**name your challenge**). Here are examples from the book: Despair, hopelessness, sadness, anger, anxiety, fear, heartache, guilt, failure, fright, and shame. I need help. Oh God, please hear my prayer! Help me! Calm my mind and spirit. I trust that you heard me. Thank you for hearing from me. So let it be.

## *Prayer #4:*
## *Thanksgiving*

Dear God/Yahweh/My Creator,

I heard that I am supposed to give you thanks for all things, so I am thanking you for everything right now. I thank you for giving me life; for meeting my needs; for protecting me from danger; (you may include other things for which you are thankful). Please save me from destruction, I pray. Thank you for listening to me. So let it be.

**NOTE:** Your Creator is no respecter of people. In your prayers, you are slowly getting to know your Creator on a personal level. I am sure that there is a celebration going on in the heavenlies because you were willing to step out and trust the process in Faith. I am proud of you. You are royalty because a Royal Priest created you.

This is phenomenal, can you imagine? This is how special you are, prince, and princess. Do not believe the hype that you are not enough. It is a lie; you are enough! You are the future. Fight with the help of your Creator for your mind. Satan is selling you worldly things (i.e., sex, drugs, and material things) to wreck your life. While there is nothing wrong with having sex, it should be done in the right context of marriage; this is how your Creator intended it to be.

Using drugs is never a good thing for your mind. It alters your thinking and makes way for Satan to control you. The things that you thought were bad are now looked at as good. I am encouraging you to fight for your mind.

# INTERNATIONAL RESOURCES & EMERGENCY NUMBERS

## Part 1

United States 988 Suicide & Crisis Lifeline 24/7 Crisis Services: 988 lifeline.org/. If you or someone you know is struggling or in crisis, help is available.

Call or text **988** or chat **988lifeline.org**. Veterans, press 1 when calling.

**911 if you are within the United States**. Become familiar with your local emergency number.

**United States Crisis Text Line:**

**Text Hello to 741741.** Crisis Text Line fields messages about suicidal thoughts, abuse, sexual assault, depression, anxiety, bullying and more.

United States **National Suicide Prevention Hotline**: **1-800-273-8255**

United States **Youth Line**: **Text teen2teen to 839863, or call 1-877-968-8491**

United States **Child Help National Child Abuse Hotline**: **call or text 1-800-422-4453**

United States **N**ational **Domestic Violence Hotline**:
**Text "START" to 88788 or call 1-800-799-7233**

United States **www.cnet** Wellness - 13 suicide and crisis intervention hotlines to call or text when you need help.
Sarah Mitroff, Sept. 1, 2021, 11:41 am PT.

United States **Veterans Crisis Line**

Send a text to **838255**

United States **Vets4Warriors**
1-855-838-8255

United States **SAMHSA Treatment Referral Hotline (Substance Abuse) 1-800-662-HELP (4357)**

United States for Encouragement
800-633-3446

https://needencouragement.com/free-christian-counseling/

United States **RAINN National Sexual Assault Hotline**
1-800-656-4673

Thrive Counseling
Phone: (876) 833-5094
Email: thrivecounselingjamaica@gmail.com

# INTERNATIONAL RESOURCES & EMERGENCY NUMBERS

## *Part 2*

- Befrienders.org – worldwide
  https://www.befrienders.org
  Befrienders **Worldwide** - Global Suicide Prevention

- https://www.moh.gov.jm › mental-health – Jamaica

- https://www.jampsych.com/copy-of-about-us - Jamaica
  https://www.bellevuehospital.org.jm

- Bellevue Hospital | The Bellevue Hospital provide care for
  mentally ill ...Jamaica

The hospital's **Emergency** Room offers assessment, treatment and admission of all psychiatric emergencies guided by hospital admission policy. ...

Join us on a visit to learn about **mental health services**
Appointments & Referrals
Tel: (876) 928-1380-7
Time: Mon - Fri. 8am - 6pm
Patient FAQs - Answers to frequently asked questions about ...

- Netherlands Suicide Prevention
  Website: www.113.nl

- National Suicide Prevention Lifeline (USA
  Website: www.suicidepreventionlifeline.org

- Lifeline International
  Website: https://www.lifeline.org.au/

- Child Helpline International
  Website: http://www.childhelplineinternational.org/where-
  we-work/

- International Federation of Telephone Emergency Services –
  IFOTES
  Website: http://www.ifotes.org/members/full-members

- Telephone Helplines Association (UK)
  Website: http://search.helplines.org/

- Teléfono de la Esperanza
  Website: http://www.telefonodelaesperanza.org/

- Papyrus (UK)
  Website: http://www.papyrus-uk.org/

- American Association of Suicidology – AAS
  Website: www.suicidology.org

- Canadian Association of Suicide Prevention – CASP
  Website: http://suicideprevention.ca/

- International Association for Suicide Prevention – IASP
  Website: http://www.iasp.info/

# INTERNATIONAL RESOURCES & EMERGENCY NUMBERS

### Part 3

- **Malatavie Prévention – Centre d'étude et de prévention du suicide -** Website: http://ceps.hug-ge.ch/centre-d-etude-et-de-prevention-du-suicide

- St. Andrew Parish 17 Ripon Rd
  Kingston, Jamaica
  876-830-6017
  cbtcaribbean@gmail.com

- **Jamaica** Ministry's **Mental Health** and Suicide Prevention Helpline - 888-NEW-LIFE (888-639-5433).

- Mental Health | Ministry of Health – Trinidad
  St. Ann's Psychiatric Hospital
  St. Ann's Road St. Ann's **Trinidad**
  Tel. (868) 624-1151 Opening hours: 24 hours

### Where can I find more information?
For a list of other **mental health** facility locations, please see the section below.

- **https://needencouragement.com**

- **https://chatnow.org**

- **https://www.onlinetherapy.com -**
  (Online Christian Counseling – Online Therapy)

- **https://www.christianchat.net**

- **https://www.hopefortheheart.org/counseling/**

- **Call us 1-800-488-HOPE (4673)**
  Monday through Friday, 8 a.m.-1:30 a.m. CST;
  Closed weekends

- Línea end Español **1-855-867-0824**

- **CHAT** – Need Encouragement.com -
  **https://needencouragement.com**

- Churchofjesuschrist.org

- **https://hittinghomeministry.com**
  (Coaching 24 hr. Marriage Counseling)
  https://www.regain.us (24 hr. free counseling hotline) -
  Not for ongoing services

- **https://blessedbeliever.com**

- **https://samaritanshope.org** (24/7 Helpline – Samaritans)

- https://www.christian.com

# ABOUT THE AUTHOR

**Judith Wilson** holds a Bachelor of Science in Social Work and a Master of Education with a concentration in Mental Health She is the author of the best–selling book, *Passion, Heartache, and Inspiration: A Collection of Poems,* and a public speaker who is not limited to these titles.

She draws inspiration from listening intently to the experiences of others, her own experiences and most importantly, her Creator. She absolutely loves her Creator and knows the importance of allowing him to lead and guide her life.

Judith enjoys writing, playing golf, nature walks, watching American football and her all-time favorite—soccer, just to name a few. She strives daily to be a beacon of light to others.

Made in the USA
Middletown, DE
29 October 2023

41446654R00076